IMAGES
of America

JOHN F. KENNEDY SITES
IN DALLAS–FORT WORTH

Mark Doty and John H. Slate

D1452441

ARCADIA
PUBLISHING

Published by Arcadia Publishing
Charleston, South Carolina

Printed in the United States of America

Library of Congress Control Number: 2013937876

For all general information, please contact Arcadia Publishing:
Telephone 843-853-2070
Fax 843-853-0044
E-mail sales@arcadiapublishing.com
For customer service and orders:
Toll-Free 1-888-313-2665

Visit us on the Internet at www.arcadiapublishing.com

To the preservers of history in the Metroplex; to Jerry and Lottie Doty, whose first date was on that fateful November day; to Lucinda, Ruby, and Henry Slate for their love and patience.

IMAGES
of America

JOHN F. KENNEDY SITES
IN DALLAS–FORT WORTH

CONTENTS

ACKNOWLEDGMENTS

Very special thanks to the *Dallas Morning News* and Jerome Sims. The authors wish to thank the following individuals and institutions for their contributions to this book: Dallas Park and Recreation Department; City Secretary's Office, City of Dallas; Willis Winters; Dallas Heritage Village; Evelyn Montgomery; the Sixth Floor Museum at Dealey Plaza; Megan Bryant; Sally Rodriguez; Trent Williams; Jeff Dunn; the Library of Congress Prints and Photographs Division; Lockheed Martin Aeronautics Company; 7th Bomb Wing B-36 Association; Downtown Fort Worth, Inc.; US Air Force Musicians Association; Laurie Monroe/Estate of Owen Day; River Oaks Public Library; University of North Texas Libraries; Dallas Firefighters Museum; Texas/ Dallas History and Archives, Dallas Public Library; Dallas Historical Society; John F. Kennedy Presidential Library and Museum; University of Texas Southwestern Medical School Archives; and Ed Zabel.

INTRODUCTION

No one living in North Texas in 1963 could have imagined how the course of history would change on a November day in Dallas. A day that started with hope and energy for many Texans ended with sadness and shame, much of it displayed publicly on television and in print media around the world. Scarred by the events of November 22–24, 1963, Dallas and the Fort Worth area have taken a half-century to come to grips with one of the darkest events in American history: the assassination of Pres. John F. Kennedy.

Commonly known at the Metroplex, the Dallas–Fort Worth area had a population of 679,684 in 1963. Today, the population is nearly two million. Dallas, the "Big D," and Fort Worth, "Where the West Begins," both have long and colorful histories that have been recounted in stories about the Old West, gunfighters, cattle drives, and 20th-century bandits Bonnie and Clyde. Yet, much of this was overshadowed by the Kennedy tragedy, and along with it came a begrudging acceptance of the responsibility of preserving the history of this event. By the late 1980s, Dallas came to understand its place in history, though the struggle continues to preserve houses, structures, and landscapes with historical importance.

Some of the events of that weekend occurred in very public spaces. Others happened in shadowy apartments and on city streets. Surprisingly, the majority of sites associated with that day can still be visited in the avenues and neighborhoods of the greater Dallas–Fort Worth region. While many of the sites are well known and well traveled, it is hoped that the reader will take the time to see the less-visited and less-viewed places that played a role in the larger story.

President Kennedy himself had a keen sense of the significance and importance of historical preservation in understanding history. In October 1963, just a month before his assassination, the president recognized delegates to the 17th annual meeting of the National Trust for Historic Preservation. In his speech, the president commended the organization's efforts to preserve historical sites and cultivate an awareness of the country's past, saying, "What you are attempting to do and what interests me, of course, is trying to maintain and keep alive in this country a very lively sense of our past . . . making it possible for those who come now and perhaps can only catch American history through seeing and feeling it, giving them some sense of what a great procession this has been."

This book is a small reminder of what happened that weekend, and, hopefully, an admonishment to ensure that future generations can trace the footsteps and tire tracks of our past.

One

FORT WORTH

On November 12, 1963, Pres. John F. Kennedy held an important planning session for the upcoming election year. At the meeting, he underscored the importance of winning Florida and Texas and revealed his plans to visit both states in the next two weeks. His wife, Jacqueline Bouvier Kennedy, always a draw, would accompany him on the trip through Texas.

On November 21, the president and first lady departed on Air Force One for a two-day, five-city tour of Texas. After stops in San Antonio and Houston, the president flew on to Fort Worth, home to a large share of the country's defense aircraft industry. Kennedy's speeches in Fort Worth were an important gesture to the city's business community and to the burgeoning defense industry in Texas, as well as a nod to the Air Force tactical bombing wings headquartered at Carswell Air Force Base.

Air Force One landed at Carswell Air Force Base in rainy Fort Worth on Thursday, November 21, 1963, at 11:30 p.m. Originally known as Tarrant Field, it operated from 1942 to 1994 as a an Air Force strategic air command base. It is named after Medal of Honor recipient Maj. Horace S. Carswell Jr. For most of its operational lifetime, the base supported strategic bombing groups and wings. Today, the base is known as Naval Air Station Joint Reserve Base Fort Worth/Carswell Field and is operated by the Navy. Below, pilots and crewmen stand around the first Convair B-58 airplane upon its arrival at Carswell Air Force Base. The Carswell tower is in the background. (Above, 7th Bomb Wing B-36 Association; below, Lockheed Martin Aeronautics Company.)

Carswell Air Force Base was where the presidential entourage arrived and departed from Fort Worth. After the overnight stay and early morning speeches, the president and first lady traveled back to Carswell to board Air Force One. In this photograph, the Barksdale Air Force Base Band (745th) plays a "send off" formation for the president. (United States Air Force Musicians Association.)

In this rare and blurry news film, Carswell airmen and personnel greet the Kennedys as they leave for Dallas. (Sixth Floor Museum at Dealey Plaza.)

The Hotel Texas, designed by Sanguinet and Staats, opened in 1921. William Monnig, W.C. Stripling, Amon Carter Sr., and other civic leaders formed the Citizens Hotel Company in 1919 to finance and build the showcase hotel for Fort Worth, at a cost of $3 million. The hotel originally was to be named the Winfield for local entrepreneur Winfield Scott, but it instead opened as the Texas Hotel. (University of North Texas Libraries.)

During their stay at Hotel Texas, the president and Mrs. Kennedy discovered that the art on the walls and the sculptures in their suite were not reproductions, but original works by world-famous artists that were assembled from local private collections specifically for the Kennedys' brief stay. The Kennedys called to thank the art organizer, Ruth Carter Johnson, for the miniature exhibit. Artists represented included Thomas Eakins, Franz Kline, Henry Moore, Pablo Picasso, and Vincent van Gogh, among others. (Owen Day/Danna Day Henderson Papers.)

Cold rain hit the Metroplex on the morning of Friday, November 22, 1963. In spite of the weather, a crowd assembled outside the hotel, hoping to see the president. Kennedy gave two speeches in Fort Worth that morning, the first in a parking lot across the street from the hotel, and the second to a crowd of hundreds inside the hotel ballroom. Seen here beside Kennedy are Sen. Ralph Yarborough and Congressman Jim Wright. (*Dallas Morning News*.)

Texas political dignitaries, some donning raincoats, accompanied the president outside to the waiting crowd. Seen here from left to right are Fort Worth mayor Bayard Friedman; Sen. Ralph Yarborough; Gov. John Connally; Vice Pres. Lyndon B. Johnson; and President Kennedy. (*Dallas Morning News.*)

Despite Secret Service objections, the president took the time to deliver remarks to the drenched but appreciative audience. The president complimented his admirers, saying, "Fort Worth has no faint hearts." Among other things, he talked about the importance of our military defense, Fort Worth's role in the aircraft industry, and his continued interest in space exploration. (*Dallas Morning News.*)

Returning to the hotel, he delivered his remarks at the chamber of commerce breakfast, a $100-per-plate fundraiser. Among those at the head table were Congressman Jim Wright; Vice President Johnson; Governor Connally; and Mayor Friedman. In the audience were many governmental, municipal, civic, business, academic, and community leaders. The indoor speech more formally touched upon the same topics as his outdoor speech. (*Dallas Morning News*.)

In his indoor speech (below), the president quipped, "I'm the man who accompanied Mrs. Kennedy to Paris. And I'm getting that same sensation as I travel around Texas. Nobody wonders what Lyndon and I wear." (John F. Kennedy Presidential Library, Cecil Stoughton.)

15

The Kennedys left the hotel, and the presidential motorcade crawled down Main Street, viewed by thousands. Elected officials followed en route to Carswell Air Force Base and then on to Dallas for the next scheduled engagement. (Left, John F. Kennedy Presidential Library, Cecil Stoughton; below, *Dallas Morning News*.)

En route to Carswell Air Force Base, the presidential entourage was greeted by thousands along an approximately nine-mile motorcade route through the neighborhoods of west Fort Worth. (Both, River Oaks Public Library.)

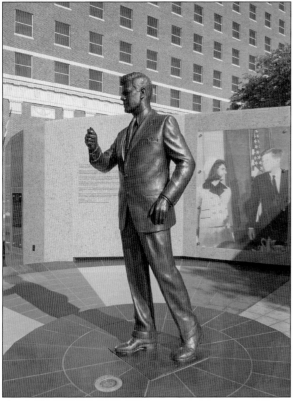

Many citizens felt that proper recognition was never given to Kennedy's final stop and speeches. Finally, 49 years later, in 2012, a public-private partnership in Fort Worth completed a decade-long effort to create a permanent exhibit to honor the president. The JFK Tribute in Fort Worth has at its center a heroic-scale bronze sculpture of President Kennedy created by sculptor Lawrence Ludtke. The sculpture stands within an elegant granite plaza featuring photographic displays and selected quotes from a number of Kennedy's historic speeches. (Both, Downtown Fort Worth, Inc.)

The JFK Tribute is located in Fort Worth's General Worth Square, at the southeast corner of Main and Eighth Streets and immediately adjacent to the former Hotel Texas (now the Hilton Hotel), where the president and Mrs. Kennedy spent his last night. The square, a parking lot at the time, was the site of President Kennedy's outdoor remarks that morning. The JFK Tribute was dedicated in a large ceremony on November 8, 2012. With additional funding coming from the City of Fort Worth Parks Department, Downtown Fort Worth Initiatives, Inc., spearheaded basic improvements to the park, including new lighting, electrical repairs, brickwork, irrigation, and seating. (Downtown Fort Worth, Inc.)

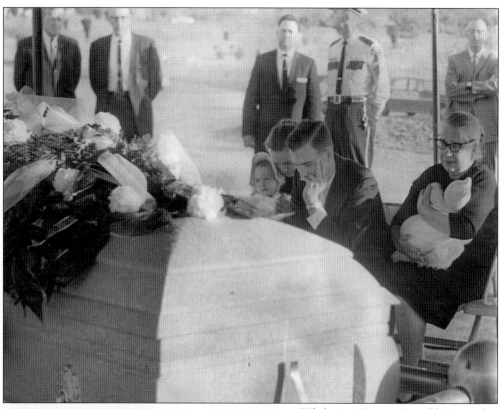

While Lee Harvey Oswald, Kennedy's shooter, grew up in several places, Fort Worth is most identified as his hometown. Oswald's family gathered the day after his death to bury him in Rose Hill Cemetery. Above, the Oswald family, including his widow, children, brother, and mother, sit beside the casket. His grave is seen at left. (Both, *Dallas Morning News*.)

This building on Camp Bowie Boulevard is the one-time home of Lee Harvey Oswald. Before that, it was the officers' club for the World War I Camp Bowie Army base. It was a boardinghouse when Oswald lived in it with his mother while attending Arlington Heights High School. Later, it was a restaurant and bar called the Rangoon Raquet Club. (Dallas Municipal Archives.)

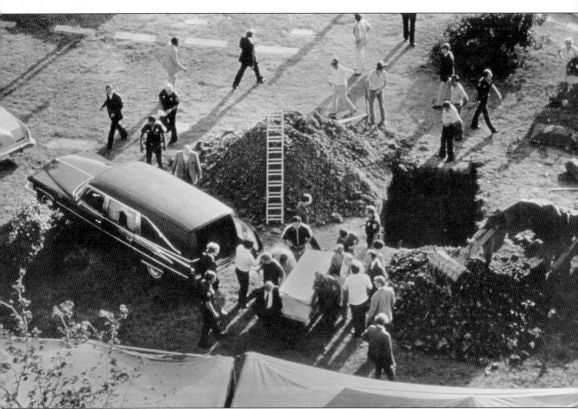

Many critics have not accepted the conclusions of the Warren Commission and have proposed a number of other theories, including that Oswald conspired with others, was not involved at all, or was framed. In October 1981, with his widow's support, Oswald's grave was opened to test a theory that during Oswald's stay in the Soviet Union he was replaced with a Soviet double. Some believed that it was this double, not Oswald himself, who killed Kennedy and who was buried in Oswald's grave. However, dental records positively identified the exhumed corpse as Oswald's, and a unique surgical scar of his was also present. (*Dallas Morning News.*)

Two

LOVE FIELD AND THE
PRESIDENTIAL MOTORCADE

After a short flight from Carswell Air Force Base in Fort Worth, Air Force One arrived at Dallas Love Field airport to begin that portion of Kennedy's Texas visit. After leaving Love Field, the motorcade was to follow a meandering 10-mile route that would end at the Dallas Trade Mart, the location of a luncheon with Dallas civic and business leaders. The 45 minutes allotted for the motorcade would allow maximum exposure to Dallas crowds for not only the president but also Vice Pres. Lyndon Johnson and Texas governor John Connally.

Established by the Army as a flying installation in October 1917, Love Field was purchased by the city in 1928, and the first terminal for commercial air passengers was completed in 1929. Named after Army flyer Moss Love, who was killed in 1913 in an accident in San Diego, Love Field continues to expand as the primary aviation facility in Dallas. (Dallas Municipal Archives.)

Airline service first came to Love on June 1, 1929, when Delta Air Service operated the first passenger flight from Dallas to Jackson, Mississippi, with stops in Shreveport and Monroe, Louisiana. This 1956 image of a Fokker F-32 passenger airplane sitting on a dirt runway shows the 1940 terminal constructed at the end of George Coker Circle, just off Lemmon Avenue. (*Dallas Morning News.*)

By the time the new terminal was built in 1958, Love Field was the largest airport in the Southwest. Designed by Jack Corgan, the state-of-the-art building featured three concourses with moving sidewalks and the Luau Room Restaurant above the main lobby. (*Dallas Morning News.*)

Interested citizens began to flock to the area around Love Field to gain a view of Air Force One as it began its descent. After finally landing at 11:40 a.m., Air Force One parked just off the Love Field terminal's east concourse. (*Dallas Morning News*.)

A beaming first lady and President Kennedy are greeted by a committee headed by Dallas mayor Earle Cabell, as Texas governor John Connally and his wife, Nellie, descend the stairs behind them. (*Dallas Morning News*.)

After greeting local dignitaries and receiving a bouquet of red roses, the Kennedys, breaking from the schedule and their Secret Service escort, crossed the pavement to acknowledge the citizens who had come to Love Field. (*Dallas Morning News.*)

Pan American Airways employees and other interested Love Field workers were also afforded a close-up view of the president and the first lady. (John F. Kennedy Presidential Library, Cecil Stoughton.)

Vice Pres. Lyndon B. Johnson and Lady Bird Johnson are seen here behind and to the right of the first couple, as they make their way to the teeming crowd at Love Field. (*Dallas Morning News.*)

Dallasites greet the president and the first lady as they walked the length of the Love Field fence. (*Dallas Morning News.*)

A visibly happy first lady continued to shake hands and greet the well-wishers who clamored for a touch or a peek at the couple. (*Dallas Morning News.*)

Signs and placards of all shapes and sizes, including two that playfully made light of the president's pronunciation of the word "vigor," were brought to Love Field by excited Dallas citizens. There were also a few signs that expressed different viewpoints. (*Dallas Morning News.*)

At 11:52 a.m., the Kennedys climbed in the backseat, with Gov. John Connally and his wife, Nellie, in the front, as their black Lincoln left Love Field and made its way to the designated motorcade route to downtown. (*Dallas Morning News*.)

Rain clouds in the distance had cleared out of the vicinity, making way for the brilliant November sun. The clear weather allowed for the top of the Lincoln to be put down, giving citizens along the motorcade full view of the president and the rest of the car's occupants. (*Dallas Morning News*.)

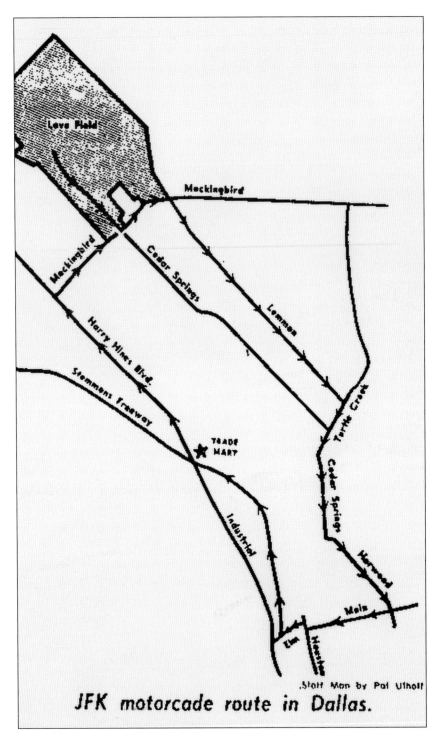

JFK motorcade route in Dallas.

This map of the motorcade route showed how the procession made its way from Love Field along Lemmon Avenue, down Turtle Creek Boulevard, onto Cedar Springs Road, and then into the main downtown core. An estimated 200,000 people lined the streets along the way. (*Dallas Morning News.*)

This young lady and other supporters of President Kennedy were some of the first people to be seen along the motorcade as the procession made its way out of the Love Field entrance north onto Mockingbird Boulevard. (*Dallas Morning News.*)

A nun keeps order among her charges at St. Ann's Catholic School, who lined Harwood Street as the motorcade passed on its way into downtown. President Kennedy stopped to greet the schoolchildren, one of two unplanned stops along the route. The epicenter of Catholic life in Little Mexico, the school closed in 1975. The building in the background was demolished in 2004. (*Dallas Morning News.*)

The passengers on a city bus were afforded a bird's-eye view of the motorcade as it passed through the intersection of Main and Ervay Streets. The flagship Neiman-Marcus store is visible in the top center. (*Dallas Morning News.*)

The surging crowd continued to build as the motorcade continued west along Main Street. In this photograph, taken at the intersection of Main and Akard Streets, Walgreen's is on the right, on the ground floor of the Gulf States Building, and Florsheim Shoe Store is on the left, anchoring the ground floor of the Adolphus Hotel tower. (*Dallas Morning News.*)

Victor Hugo King took this photograph, a close-up view of the Kennedys and the Connallys as the motorcade continued down Main Street. Right before making a left turn from Houston Street onto Elm Street, Nellie Connally, impressed with the large and enthusiastic crowds along the downtown streets, turned to the backseat and said, "Mr. President, you certainly cannot say that Dallas does not love you." (Library of Congress.)

This iconic Cecil Stoughton photograph shows Pres. Lyndon B. Johnson back aboard Air Force One at Love Field, taking the oath of office from judge Sarah T. Hughes. Others in the photograph include the new first lady, Lady Bird Johnson; Dallas police chief Jesse Curry, with his face hidden by Johnson's raised hand; the secretary to President Kennedy, Evelyn Lincoln, mostly hidden behind Mrs. Kennedy; Jacqueline Kennedy; and Congressman Jack Brooks of Texas. (John F. Kennedy Presidential Library, Cecil Stoughton.)

A little before 2:00 p.m., less than three hours after landing at Love Field, onlookers watch President John F. Kennedy's casket loaded onto Air Force One. Among them are Lawrence "Larry" O'Brien, a special assistant to the president; Jacqueline Kennedy; Dave Powers, also a special assistant to the president; and Chester V. Clifton, a military aide to the president. (John F. Kennedy Presidential Library, Cecil Stoughton.)

Jacqueline Kennedy boards Air Force One just after her husband's casket was loaded onboard. (John F. Kennedy Presidential Library, Cecil Stoughton.)

Federal judge Sarah T. Hughes is seen here in her car after administering the oath of office to Lyndon B. Johnson aboard Air Force One at Love Field. (*Dallas Morning News.*)

Three

DEALEY PLAZA

Dealey Plaza is the second-most visited historic site in Texas, after the Alamo. Known as the Front Door of Dallas, the park rests on a bluff near the Trinity River, where a natural low-water crossing was identified in 1841 by Dallas's founder, John Neely Bryan. The ford was the site of Bryan's cabin as well as the first ferry and bridge over the Trinity River. John Neely Bryan's cabin was erected of cedar logs on the east bank of the river, near what is now Elm Street in Dealey Plaza.

Besides being a city park, Dealey Plaza is the focal point of the triple underpass traffic diverter and is flanked by a number of historic buildings, including the 1892 Dallas County Courthouse, the Dallas County Records Building, the Dallas County Criminal Courts Building, and the former Texas School Book Depository.

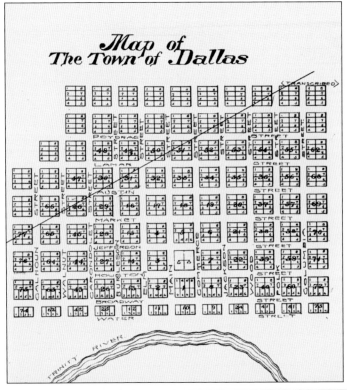

Map of The Town of Dallas

John Neely Bryan (1810–1874), the founder of Dallas, was the first white settler in the area and constructed a simple structure in November 1841 at the forks of the Trinity River, on the east side of a natural ford that was at the intersection of two existing American Indian traces. In 1844, he persuaded J.P. Dumas to survey and plat the townsite of Dallas. When Dallas was selected as the county seat, Bryan donated land for the courthouse as well as 90 town lots. At left, the earliest existing map of the area, from 1850, shows the future Dealey Plaza area. Below is a replica of Bryan's cabin. (Both, Dallas Municipal Archives.)

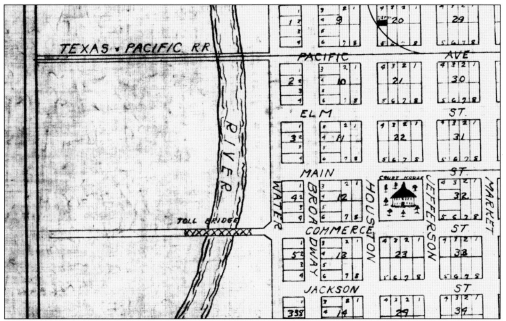

Before the rerouting of the Trinity River in 1928, there were two more parallel streets west of Houston Street before the river. This 1882 map shows Broadway, an unpaved road that provided a path for both commercial and passenger railroad tracks. Water Street was a dirt footpath fronting the river at the time. (Dallas Municipal Archives.)

In 1872, Herman Brosius created a bird's-eye view of Dallas that is amazingly accurate in its details. This is an enlarged view of what is now Dealey Plaza. The courthouse square is in the center, with Commerce Street to the south. A flour mill faces Broadway, to the north of Sarah Cockrell's iron bridge. (Library of Congress.)

No. 767
Toll Bridge over the Trinity
in 1872-Dallas, Texas.

The bridges across the Trinity River have always been essential in unifying Dallas. The first, a covered wooden toll bridge, was built in 1855 by Alexander Cockrell and extended from Commerce Street. The second Commerce Street Bridge, built in 1871 and seen here in 1872, was an iron-bowstring toll bridge that was operated by Cockrell's widow until it was purchased by Dallas County in 1882. The building to the left is the Crutchfield House Hotel, and immediately to the right of the bridge is its toll both. (*Dallas Morning News.*)

Dallas Fire Department Station No. Five, on Houston Street between Main and Elm Streets, was typical of the kinds of buildings on the two blocks that became Dealey Plaza. The station, built in 1890, is seen above around 1905 and below in an undated photograph. The entire block was razed in 1934 to make way for the triple underpass and Dealey Plaza. (Above, Dallas Firefighters Museum; below, *Dallas Morning News*.)

The Dealey Plaza area is within a natural floodplain of the Trinity River, and, until the levees were completed in 1932, it was perpetually in danger of flooding. Major floods, especially those in 1908 and 1935, were destructive. In this 1908 photograph, the Commerce Street Bridge is partially washed out, severing Oak Cliff and West Dallas from the eastern half of the city. (Library of Congress.)

Plagued by nearly annual flooding, Dallas tamed the river through a series of levees, paid for by the citizens of Dallas through a bond program passed in 1928. The city's planning interests recommended a new union train terminal and the consolidation of railway tracks in the central business district. These improvements, along with the realignment of the river itself, directly enabled the development of the triple underpass and Dealey Plaza. (Dallas Municipal Archives.)

Dallas Union Terminal, also known as Union Station, was built in 1914, just two blocks south of the future plaza. In 1933, a site was chosen for a permanent postal service substation convenient to Union Station. It was across from the courthouse, adjacent to the eastern approach of the Commerce Street Bridge. In a few short years, it became the southern boundary of Dealey Plaza. (*Dallas Morning News.*)

With the realignment of the Trinity River and the construction of a new system of bridges to span it, attention turned to the creation of a new western entrance to the city. Two square blocks were targeted, seen here in 1931. The river was moved almost a quarter mile west. The 1916 Commerce Street Bridge is also seen here. (Dallas Municipal Archives.)

Two Blocks Where Dallas Was Born to Be Cleared for Million-Dollar Project

Northwest corner of Commerce and Houston which once housed

the city's most important business establishments

400 Commerce, once the site of the finest building in North Texas

This is the site of the historic Crutchfield House. Title to entire Houston street frontage was acquired by Thomas Crutchfield, the proprietor...

Remnants of once sumptuous woodwork, adorning bar mirrors of Apperson's New Idea Saloon

Finger prints of workers who made brick by hand for Dallas buildings fifty years ago plainly visible on walls

Southwest corner Houston and Main original lot 1 block 1 city of Dallas. Original construction of white rock showing through the later coat.

Old Mill structure Elm and Broadway

Main street looking west from Houston. This street was once the terminal of Tom Marsalis' steam railroad connecting Dallas and Oak Cliff...

Time worn, but stanch, the two blocks of aging walls which closely succeeded the first log structures of the early business district of Dallas on the two blocks bounded by Commerce, Elm, Houston and Broadway, will go down within a few weeks with accord the homage due them as the cradle of a mighty city. In the buildings Dallasites of half a century ago and longer did virtually all the shopping transacted their law and real estate business and carried on the activities incident to a rapidly flow...

The two blocks slated for leveling contained some of the earliest buildings in Dallas. While the history of the area was acknowledged, the buildings themselves were considered ghosts of Dallas's past. In September 1934, on the eve of demolition, the *Dallas Morning News* published this profile of the historic buildings. (*Dallas Morning News*.)

46

The ambitious public works project that was eventually named Dealey Plaza required the reconfiguration of the three main streets in downtown Dallas into a six-lane boulevard on the western edge of the central business district. This 1936 aerial view shows how the three streets converged to pass under the railroad tracks that fed into Union Station, in the upper right. West of the tracks, the new thoroughfare crossed the relocated channel of the Trinity River on the new Commerce Street Viaduct and then continued westward to Fort Worth. This massive undertaking was referred to as the Elm-Main-Commerce underpass, or, more simply, as the triple underpass. (*Dallas Morning News*.)

Beginning in November 1934, buildings were razed at a rapid pace to construct the triple underpass. These two images show the amount of work that had to be done. (Above, Dallas Public Library; below, *Dallas Morning News*.)

Excavation beneath existing train tracks was the first step during construction, and, by June 1935, the massive concrete walls and overhead steel beams that would support the new tracks were in place. A Texas & Pacific freight train was the first to pass over the bridge when it was completed five months later. (Dallas Public Library.)

Following excavation and the construction of the overpass, 65,000 cubic yards of earth were removed between the new bridge and Houston Street. Elm, Main, and Commerce Streets were regraded to slope down 24 feet. The convergence of these three streets under the bridge formed the triple underpass. (Dallas Municipal Archives.)

The railroad overpass was finished in November 1935, prior to any other work. In this view, looking east toward the bridge with downtown buildings beyond, solid earth can be seen on the far side of the three automobile tunnels. The *Dallas Morning News* commented that the modernistic design was "strikingly illustrated" and was reminiscent of the pylons and buildings at the 1933 Chicago World's Fair. (Dallas Public Library.)

On May 1, 1936, Dallas celebrated the opening of the $1-million public works project. Bands entertained prior to the dedication ceremonies, presided over by chairman Harry Hines (lower right). Festivities concluded with a street dance and a square dance contest. This event was a prelude to the Texas Centennial Exposition, which opened the following week with a massive parade down Main Street witnessed by over 50,000 people. (*Dallas Morning News.*)

The physical character of Dealey Plaza today was largely determined by a second beautification program, completed in 1941. The master plan was prepared by Hare & Hare, landscape architects from Kansas City. The main design features were twin concrete peristyles and plazas located behind the National Youth Administration–constructed reflecting pools and pylons along Houston Street and matching shelters and pergolas in the northwest and southwest corners of the site. This project was built by the Works Progress Administration (WPA) at a total cost of $92,298. Of that amount, $37,284 was contributed by the park board. (Dallas Municipal Archives.)

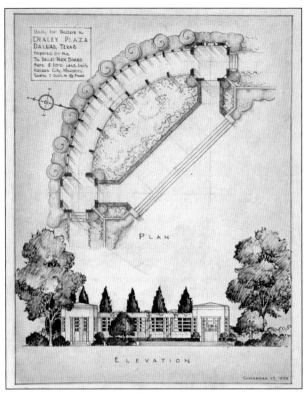

Hare & Hare's design for each corner of Dealey Plaza included covered shelters connected by a curving, open-air pergola. The modernistic design of these structures complimented the Art Deco styling of the triple underpass. A diagonal plaza with steps down to the grass lawn connected each pair of shelters. These important features of Hare & Hare's design were restored to their original condition by the Dallas Park and Recreation Department in 2013. (Both, Dallas Municipal Archives.)

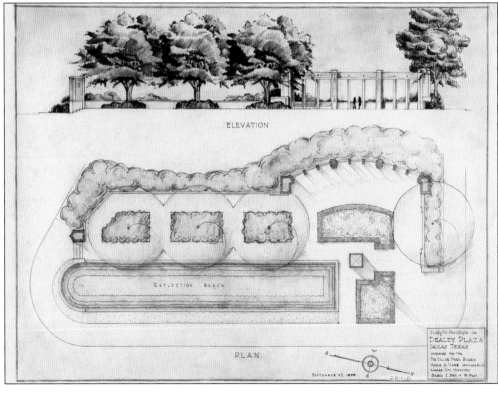

The WPA began work on Dealey Plaza in March 1940, completing the project 11 months later in February 1941. In this view of the construction, taken in July 1940, concrete work on the two shelters is largely complete, and WPA workers are beginning to erect the wood frame for the curving pergola. (*Dallas Morning News.*)

Dealey Plaza Shelter House Starts Taking Form

Beautification of Dealey Plaza, gateway through the Triple Underpass to the city from the west, has progressed so a substantial idea can be obtained of how the $92,298 city-WPA project is going to look. Work began March 10, is scheduled for completion about Nov. 1. This is one of the two curving shelter-house and pergola structures that will grace the corners nearest the tracks. Opposite them, on the courthouse side of the park, will be a pair of similarly curved structures called peristyles, one behind each of the two present reflecting basins. A complete landscaping program, costing $10,000, will involve a solid carpet of grass between the broad, curving sidewalks that will connect all points on the plaza, with a host of flower ornamentations and many cedar elms, red cedars and live oaks.

A 12-foot-high bronze statue of George B. Dealey was dedicated at Dealey Plaza on November 14, 1949. Dealey championed the levees and other civic improvements. The sculpture replaced one of the stone obelisks that had been built in this location by the National Youth Administration in 1937. The sculptor was Felix de Weldon (1907–2003), who later designed the US Marine Corps's Iwo Jima Memorial. (Dallas Historical Society.)

TRIPLE UNDERPASS PARK, HOUSTON STREET POSTOFFICE IN BACKGROUND, DALLAS, TEXAS

When the WPA completed construction of Dealey Plaza in 1941, it provided Dallas with an iconic image that was featured on numerous postcards in the 1940 and 1950s. The new gateway to Dallas was not only an innovative transportation achievement but also a beautifully landscaped parklike entrance into a vibrant and growing metropolis. (Dallas Municipal Archives.)

Today, Dealey Plaza and its surroundings look much as they did 70 years ago. Only two new buildings have been constructed during this time period: the 1955 expansion of the county records building, on the southeast corner of Elm and Houston Streets, and the new 1965 county courthouse and jail, on the southeast corner of Commerce and Houston Streets. (Dallas Municipal Archives.)

Many historical buildings flank the plaza. The John Deere Plow Company building (now at 501 Elm Street) was built in 1902 as the Kingman Implement Company, one of the most architecturally significant buildings in the West End Historic District. Also called the Dal-Tex Building, it served as the office of assassination witness Abraham Zapruder's apparel manufacturing business, Jennifer Juniors, Inc. (Dallas Heritage Village.)

Offices and Warehouse JOHN DEERE PLOW CO. Dallas, Tex.

The postcard below showcases more of the warehouse district, including the Southern Rock Island Plow Company, the John Deere building, and the Tenison Brothers Saddlery Company. This view is unique because, to the south, it shows the buildings now occupied by the Dallas County Records Building and the criminal courts building. (Jeff Dunn.)

Birds Eye View of a part of Dallas Implement & Saddlery Wholesale Houses. Dallas, Texas.

As the triple underpass project was finishing construction in 1936, the federal government demolished a third block of old buildings on Houston Street to construct a $1-million postal substation. The site of the new facility, which was designed by Lang & Witchell, bordered Dealey Plaza on the south. This view of the construction shows the recently completed triple underpass in the background. (*Dallas Morning News.*)

Two often-overlooked buildings surrounding Dealey Plaza are the railroad switching towers built by the Missouri-Kansas-Texas Railroad in 1916. Two rail yards, each with line-switching towers, were built to the north and south of the station. The north tower, seen here, was occupied by "tower man" Lee Bowers Jr. on the day of the assassination. (Dallas Municipal Archives.)

The redbrick building on the northeast corner of Dealey Plaza has stood in this location since 1901. It has had multiple owners and names over the past 114 years, the most infamous being the Texas School Book Depository, in 1963, when the motorcade of Pres. John F. Kennedy slowed to make a sharp turn from Houston Street onto Elm Street, directly in front of the building. After standing empty for many years, Dallas County purchased the building from a subsequent owner and renovated it as the county administration building in 1981. The top two floors of the structure remained empty until 1989, when the Sixth Floor Museum opened. Millions of visitors have made pilgrimages to Dealey Plaza to understand the tragic event that occurred here. This photograph was taken in November 1963, days after the assassination. Mourners are on the left side of the image, on the lawn that slopes upward to the northwest pergola. (*Dallas Morning News.*)

The Southern Rock Island Plow Company was established in 1899 as a regional branch of B.D. Buford & Company of Chicago to sell agricultural implements to the farmers of North Texas. It was the second-most profitable branch house for the company and boasted a catalog heavily dedicated to southern crops like cotton. This advertisement is from 1905. (Dallas Public Library.)

The present Southern Rock Island Plow Company building (below) was constructed in 1901 to replace the previous five-story warehouse structure, which was struck by lightning and burned in a spectacular conflagration. This photograph was taken around 1910. (*Dallas Morning News*.)

In this crime scene photograph taken by the Dallas Police Department after the assassination, the Texas School Book Depository stands in visual isolation from the other buildings that surround Dealey Plaza. This was the view that confronted the presidential motorcade on November 22, 1963, as it made the right turn from Main Street onto Houston Street. (Dallas Municipal Archives.)

These interior crime scene photographs of the depository's sixth floor show the barricade of boxes stacked around the corner window to conceal the assassin's activities from other employees in the hours preceding the assassination. (Both, Dallas Municipal Archives.)

Concealed from view within the building, the assassin positioned three boxes on the floor and windowsill (above), which allowed him to aim and fire toward the presidential limousine as it proceeded down Elm Street toward the triple underpass. (Dallas Municipal Archives.)

In this evidence photograph, a shell casing can be seen on the floor next to the brick wall under the window. (Dallas Municipal Archives.)

In 1970, D. Harold Byrd, the owner of the Texas School Book Depository, put the building up for sale. It was briefly owned by Nashville promoter Aubrey Mayhew and damaged in a fire before it returned to the Byrd family in 1972. In a bizarre twist in 2007, Mayhew attempted to sell, through online auction, the sixth-floor window from which the sniper shot the president, claiming he had removed it. Byrd's son countered, saying he owned the true window and would also auction it off to the highest bidder. After lawsuits over the ownership of the true window and the death of Mayhew in 2009, the dispute remains unsettled. (Dallas Municipal Archives.)

Next to the School Book Depository on the grassy knoll is this five-foot-tall wooden stockade fence line that is approximately 169 feet long. In 1964, the Warren Commission concluded that only three shots were fired, all from behind the president and all from the School Book Depository. In 1979, an investigation conducted by the House Assassinations Committee acknowledged that a possible fourth shot, which missed, had been fired from behind the fence. (Both, Ed Zabel.)

In 1989, the Sixth Floor Museum at Dealey Plaza added a ground-level visitors' center behind the building and an external elevator tower—very controversial with Dallas preservationists—that took visitors up to the sixth and seventh levels of the building. The museum's popularity and innovative programming has helped preserve the history of Dealey Plaza in a respectful manner. (Both, Dallas Municipal Archives.)

The end of the president's parade in Dallas was intentionally planned to end at Dealey Plaza. It was not only a convenient entrance onto Stemmons Freeway, but the plaza also provided Dallas citizens with a large gathering place from which to see and greet the president. (Dallas Municipal Archives.)

After traveling much of the length of Main Street, the motorcade turned right on Houston Street, where it would take a sharp left onto Elm Street into Dealey Plaza. After driving through the triple underpass, the motorcade was to veer to the right to take the ramp to North Stemmons Freeway to the Dallas Trade Mart, at 2100 North Stemmons Freeway. This is where the limousine turned right on Houston Street. (*Dallas Morning News.*)

The last seconds of President Kennedy's life were spent waving to cheering crowds in Dealey Plaza. Here, Secret Service agents look in the direction of the Dal-Tex Building. (*Dallas Morning News.*)

At 12:29 p.m., the presidential limousine entered Dealey Plaza. Along with the president were the first lady, Texas governor John Connally; his wife, Nellie; and a driver. Five cars followed, which included Vice Pres. Lyndon B. Johnson; his wife, Lady Bird Johnson; Sen. Ralph Yarborough; and a press corps bus. Most witnesses recall hearing three shots, with the second two distinctly closer together than the first. (Phil Willis Collection/the Sixth Floor Museum at Dealey Plaza.)

After the fatal shots, the limousine driver and police motorcycles raced at full speed to Parkland Hospital. Spectators scattered, with some hitting the ground to avoid danger and others running both away from and towards perceived shooting sources. Dallas Police Department escorts and Secret Service agents swarmed the plaza. Here, the press corps bus lags behind a few seconds. (Phil Willis Collection/the Sixth Floor Museum at Dealey Plaza.)

After the shots were fired, Bill Newman and his wife, Gayle, pressed their children to the ground along the grassy knoll, shielding them with their bodies, in one of the most indelible images of that day. (John F. Kennedy Presidential Library.)

The infamous grassy knoll is a small, sloping hill inside the plaza that was to the right of President Kennedy at the time of the shots. The name was coined by reporter Albert Merriman Smith of United Press International in his second dispatch from the radio-telephone in the press car, when he said, "Some of the Secret Service agents thought the gunfire was from an automatic weapon fired to the right rear of the president's car, probably from a grassy knoll to which police rushed." This was repeated on national television by Walter Cronkite in his second CBS News bulletin. Both these images show the fence at the top of the grassy knoll. Through the years, the fence has been a source of speculation regarding the possibility of multiple assassins. Portions of the fence have been replaced several times. (Both, Dallas Municipal Archives.)

Almost immediately, makeshift memorials to the slain president were erected in Dealey Plaza. After the initial police department crime scene investigation, wreaths and flower arrangements were assembled throughout the plaza, but especially near the north pergola, overlooking the exact spot of the president's death. These images show citizens visiting and pouring out their grief with flowers and American flags. In the image below, the George L. Allen Sr. Civil District Courthouse is under construction in the center left. (Above, Dallas Municipal Archives; below, *Dallas Morning News*.)

This *Dallas Morning News* image, taken by Clint Grant, expresses the sorrow tour that permeated Dallas for weeks. (*Dallas Morning News*.)

Floral tributes came in from around the world to express sympathy and grief. (Both, *Dallas Morning News.*)

The Secret Service, the FBI, and Warren Commission all attempted to determine the origin and timing of the shots that killed President Kennedy and wounded Governor Connally. The Secret Service staged a recreation in late 1963, seen here. The footage shot by the Secret Service was the first attempt to use motion pictures to solve the mystery of JFK's assassination. (Both, Dallas Municipal Archives.)

Opened in 1989, the Sixth Floor Museum at Dealey Plaza chronicles the assassination and legacy of Pres. John F. Kennedy; interprets the Dealey Plaza National Historic Landmark District and the John F. Kennedy Memorial Plaza; and presents contemporary culture within the context of presidential history. It has been visited by millions of people since it opened. The museum is seen here under construction in 1988. (Institutional Archives/Sixth Floor Museum at Dealey Plaza.)

Dealey Plaza is visited by more than two million people annually. Each November, visitors are drawn here to pay tribute to Kennedy, as seen in this commemoration in 1993. The School Book Depository Building was recognized in 1980 by the Texas Historical Commission as a Texas Historic Landmark. To preserve the plaza and its surrounding buildings, the federal government designated it a National Historic Landmark District in 1993. (Ronald D. Rice/Sixth Floor Museum at Dealey Plaza.)

Oliver Stone's 1991 film *JFK* was actually shot in Dealey Plaza. Dallas police rerouted traffic and closed streets for three weeks. The production spent $4 million to restore Dealey Plaza to its 1963 conditions. Stone, in an agreement with the City of Dallas, had temporary signs made and installed in Dealey Plaza. (Sixth Floor Museum at Dealey Plaza, Lovita Irby collection.)

A master plan for the restoration of Dealey Plaza was approved by the Dallas Park Board in 2003 through a combination of public and private funding. Phase I occurred in 2009. Phase II was completed in 2013, in time for the 50th anniversary commemorations of President Kennedy's death. Here, concrete is being poured to renovate sidewalks and the reflecting pools at the north end of the plaza. (Dallas Municipal Archives.)

Four

OAK CLIFF

Oak Cliff is a large neighborhood that was formerly a separate town in Dallas County, just west of the Trinity River and across from downtown and South Dallas. The City of Dallas annexed Oak Cliff in 1903, and it has since retained a distinct identity as one of Dallas's older, established neighborhoods. Oak Cliff includes houses from the early and mid-1900s, many parks, and proximity to the central business district of downtown Dallas.

It is also the site of many places connected to the Kennedy assassination, including the homes of Lee Harvey Oswald and Jack Ruby, the Texas Theater, and a number of less-visited sites such as the block where Dallas police officer J.D. Tippit was brutally murdered just after the assassination.

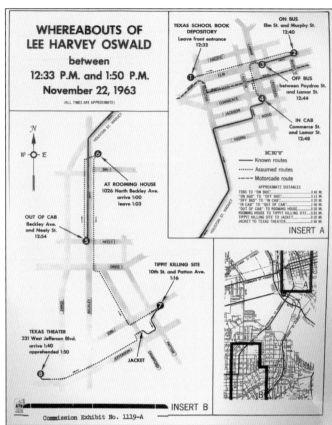

This exhibit from the Warren Commission traced Lee Harvey Oswald's whereabouts as he left the Texas School Book Depository, went over the Houston Street Viaduct, then though the North Oak Cliff neighborhood where officer J.D. Tippit was shot, at Tenth Street and Patton Avenue, and on to the Texas Theater, where he was finally captured. (*Dallas Morning News.*)

The Houston Street Viaduct was constructed over the Trinity River in 1912 to address a long-standing accessibility issue between Oak Cliff and downtown Dallas. Considered the longest concrete span in the world when it was completed, the viaduct was used by Lee Harvey Oswald to escape downtown Dallas after the assassination. (Dallas Municipal Archives.)

Apartment No. 2 in this two-story apartment building, located at the corner of Elsbeth and Davis Streets, was the home of Lee Harvey Oswald, his wife, Marina, and their daughter June for four months in 1962 and 1963. Known as the Elsbeth Court Apartments, the structure was built in 1925. The Oswalds moved out of the building in March 1963. (Dallas City Attorney's Office.)

The building at 600 Elsbeth continued to operate as an apartment building until it was completely closed down in the early 2000s, after which it remained vacant for several years. Despite efforts at revitalization by a new owner, the structure continued to deteriorate and was finally demolished by a court order on Monday, January 14, 2013. (*Dallas Morning News.*)

Lee Harvey Oswald lived in this two-story Craftsman duplex located at 214 West Neely Street during March and April 1963. The structure is still standing within the Miller-Stemmons National Register District. (Ed Zabel.)

This is the rear elevation of the two-story the duplex at 214 West Neely Street. The infamous exterior staircase accessed a second-floor living unit. (Ed Zabel.)

The 214 West Neely Street property was the location of this infamous image of Lee Harvey Oswald holding a rifle in the backyard. (Dallas Municipal Archives.)

The same staircase and backyard fence on the previous page are seen here, photographed as part of the investigation into Oswald. (Dallas Municipal Archives.)

Detective B.G. Brown of the Dallas police force stands in front of the staircase and fence in an effort to reenact the Oswald rifle image. (Dallas Municipal Archives.)

This one-story house at 1026 North Beckley Avenue has a small room that was rented to Lee Harvey Oswald for $8.00 per week from October 14 to November 21, 1963. The house stands today within the Lake Cliff Historic District. (Ed Zabel.)

A garage apartment, shown here, is behind Oswald's boarding house. Oswald arrived back at the house after crossing the Houston Street Viaduct from downtown by bus. He then left a few minutes after 1:00 p.m. (Ed Zabel.)

This house, at 621 North Marsalis Avenue, was Lee Harvey Oswald's home for one week. On October 7, 1963, he paid the week's rent of $7.00 to homeowner Mary Bledsoe. He came and went without talking and kept to himself, shuttling back and forth to Irving, where his estranged wife was about to give birth. Spooked by his odd behavior, Bledsoe declined to extend the rental. She did not see him again until November 22, 1963, when he boarded the same bus she was riding from downtown to Oak Cliff. (Ed Zabel.)

LOCATION OF EYEWITNESSES TO THE MOVEMENTS OF LEE HARVEY OSWALD IN THE VICINITY OF THE TIPPIT KILLING

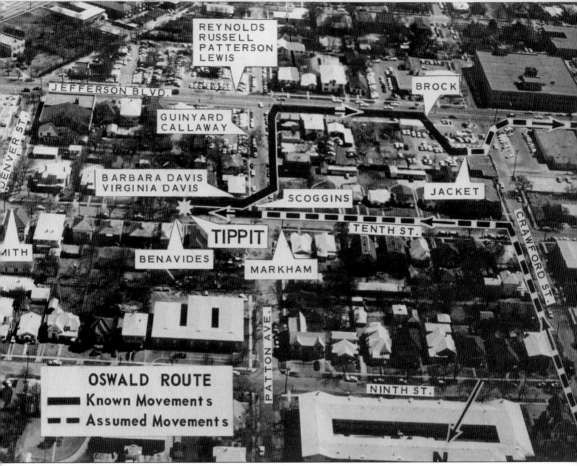

Exhibit No. 1968 from the Warren Commission tracked eyewitness locations of Lee Harvey Oswald as he made his way through East Oak Cliff to the Texas Theater after shooting police officer J.D. Tippit. (*Dallas Morning News.*)

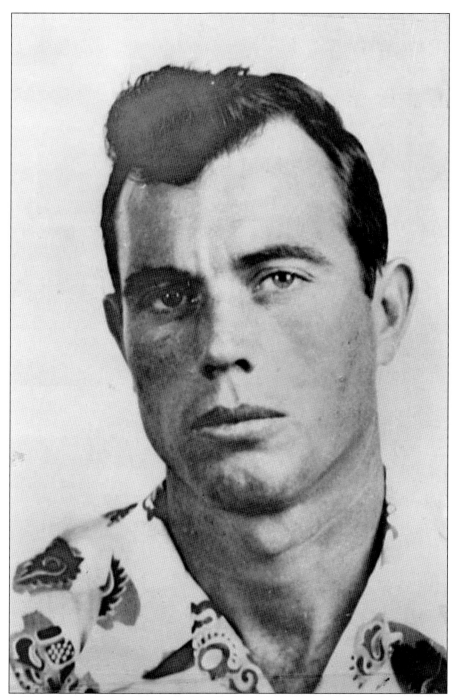

Officer J.D. Tippit, an 11-year veteran of the Dallas police force, was dispatched into Oak Cliff neighborhoods to be "at large for any emergency that comes in." Tippit was born in 1924 and grew up on his family's farm near Clarksville, Texas. He joined the Dallas Police Department in 1952. At roughly 1:15 p.m. on November 22, 1963, Tippit noticed Lee Harvey Oswald walking along Patton Avenue near Tenth Street and stopped him for questioning. Oswald then shot Tippit four times and fled along Patton Avenue towards Jefferson Boulevard. (Dallas Municipal Archives.)

The next images were taken at the scene of Officer Tippit's shooting. Single-family residences, duplexes, and other structures are seen in this photograph, which looks northeast toward the crime scene at the intersection of Tenth Street and Patton Avenue. (Dallas Municipal Archives.)

This image shows Tippit's squad car parked in front of a two-story boardinghouse on the south side of Tenth Street near Patton Avenue. (Dallas Municipal Archives.)

This photograph looks east down Tenth Street. Tippit's squad car is on the right. The murder was witnessed by several residents. (Dallas Municipal Archives.)

This image of the Tippit crime scene looks west down Tenth Street toward the intersection with Patton Avenue. The dark stain on the concrete is where Tippit fell. (Dallas Municipal Archives.)

Dallas police officers carry the casket of J.D. Tippit for interment at Laurel Land Memorial Park, at 6000 South R.L. Thornton Freeway, on November 25, 1963. An overflowing service was held at Beckley Hill Baptist Church in South Oak Cliff, with many following to observe the burial service. Officer Tippit's obituary ran on the front page of the *Dallas Morning News* on November 26. (*Dallas Morning News.*)

A Dallas police officer lays a wreath at the gravesite of J.D. Tippit as other officers and citizens stand watch. His plot is located in Section 62, Lot 1, Space 7. The public outpouring of support for Officer Tippit's family after his death was quite generous, and hundreds of thousands of dollars were raised to help his wife, Marie, support her family. (*Dallas Morning News.*)

On November 20, 2012, this state historical marker was unveiled near the corner of Tenth Street and Patton Avenue to commemorate Officer Tippit and his tragic role in the events of November 22, 1963. Members of the Tippit family, including his widow, Marie, joined the more than 200 people at the ceremony. (Mark Doty.)

Today, the intersection of Tenth Street and Patton Avenue (below) hardly resembles the neighborhood as it looked in 1963. The majority of the single-family residences and multifamily complexes have been razed over the years for new construction and sports fields for nearby Adamson High School. (Mark Doty.)

J.D. Tippit's assassin was seen running south on Patton Avenue toward Jefferson Boulevard in Oak Cliff by Warren Reynolds, who worked at his brother's used car lot at 500 Jefferson Boulevard. Reynolds was sitting in his office when he observed an individual running or walking fast down Jefferson Boulevard and then walking fast west on Jefferson. The man had a pistol in his hand, and Reynolds had previously heard shots coming from the area of Tenth Street and Patton Avenue. These photographs show the Johnny Reynolds Used Cars lot as it appeared on November 22, 1963. Reynolds called the police about the man from what was then a Texaco gas station (below). Oswald also dropped his jacket, which was later recovered by the police beside the second vehicle from the right above. (Above, Dallas Municipal Archives; below, Mark Doty.)

At the time of the assassination, Jefferson Boulevard was considered the main street in Oak Cliff. Offices, department stores and other retail establishments, restaurants, and movie theaters lined Jefferson and served the surrounding middle-class neighborhoods. Today, the street serves as a shopping district for the mainly Hispanic population of the area. (Mark Doty.)

At about 1:35 p.m., Oswald ducked into the entryway of Hardy's Shoe Store on Jefferson Boulevard in order to dodge police cars driving past. Manager Johnny Calvin Brewer followed Oswald when he left the entryway and pursued him to the Texas Theater. Although no longer the home of Hardy's Shoe Store, the storefront at 213 West Jefferson Boulevard still stands in a modified state. (Mark Doty.)

Top Ten Records, at 338 West Jefferson Boulevard, has changed very little since 1963. Several minutes before police officer J.D. Tippit was murdered at Tenth Street and Patton Avenue, he was seen at the record shop by its owner, J.W. "Dub" Stark, and a young clerk. A frequent visitor to the store, Tippit came into the shop to make a hasty telephone call of an unknown nature, got no answer, and sped away in the direction of the street where he was shortly murdered. The layout of the store is relatively unchanged after 50 years, and the telephone Tippit used is still in the same place. (Mark Doty.)

Located at 231 West Jefferson Boulevard, the Italian Renaissance–style Texas Theater opened on April 21, 1931, with *Parlor, Bedroom and Bath* starring Buster Keaton. Considered the finest picture house in Oak Cliff, the 2,000-seat theater was owned by Howard Hughes, the Texas billionaire and aviator. Moviegoers enjoyed the large, majestic auditorium, which was advertised as the first air-conditioned movie palace in Texas. (Dallas Municipal Archives.)

Although the Texas continued to screen first-rate movies, its reputation and image began to wane as newer theaters opening city-wide. The ornate facade had a thin concrete, white stucco veneer applied during the late 1940s. Lee Harvey Oswald entered the theater without paying at approximately 1:40 p.m. on November 22, 1963 in order to evade Dallas police officers. (*Dallas Morning News*.)

This interior shot of the Texas Theater lobby shows the ornate column capitals, light fixtures, and decorative wall treatments of the interior at the time of Oswald's arrest in the auditorium. All of these interior features and finishes were either removed or covered over completely with stucco in a later effort to "modernize" the theater in 1965. (Dallas Municipal Archives.)

This is an interior shot of the Texas Theater auditorium as it was right after Lee Harvey Oswald was arrested after sneaking in to hide from police officers. Notice the black-out curtains that helped filter light from the adjoining lobby. The large theater's interior theme was "Venetian Court" with special effects that created canals, buildings, and balconies. Clouds, generated with a light machine, floated over the ceiling painted as a sky with 118 twinkling stars. (Dallas Municipal Archives.)

War is Hell was playing on the screen as 15 Dallas police officers entered the theater and arrested Lee Harvey Oswald at 1:45 p.m. A Dallas police officer points to the seat where Oswald was sitting at the time of his arrest. The seat is still located within the Texas Theater and has a small plaque attached to it, marking its significance. (Dallas Municipal Archives.)

This image of Officer M.N. "Nick" McDonald, credited as the arresting officer, indicates the bloody face he received after a brief struggle with Oswald in the Texas Theater. McDonald's hand also prevented the gun Oswald was carrying from firing again. Officer McDonald passed away in January 2005. (Dallas Municipal Archives.)

In a continued effort to compete with modern theater complexes and distance the site with the Oswald arrest, the operators of the Texas removed the "TEXAS" sign and marquee along with other decorative features and covered the exterior with a more modern slip cover in 1965. The Texas continued showing first- or second-run movies until it was closed in December 1989. (Ed Zabel.)

For preparations for the film *JFK*, director Oliver Stone funded removal of the unsightly slip facade cover and a partial exterior restoration, including a temporary sign and marquee in 1991. A permanent marquee to match the historical one was installed in 2002 and a new "TEXAS" sign was erected in 2007. After several false starts for a new use, the space is enjoying a revival as a limited-run movie theater showing cult classics as well as film festivals. (Mark Doty.)

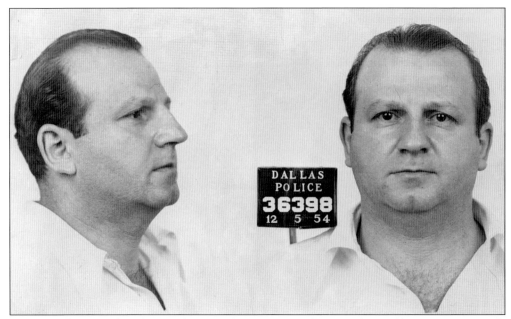

Jack Ruby (born Jacob Rubinstein) was a Chicago native who moved to Dallas in 1946. A small-time gangster and entrepreneur, Ruby owned several nightclubs in Dallas and occasionally ran afoul of the Dallas Police Department (DPD). Above is Jack Ruby's DPD mug shot from 1954. Below is a DPD mug shot from 1963, taken soon after he shot Lee Harvey Oswald. (Both, Dallas Municipal Archives.)

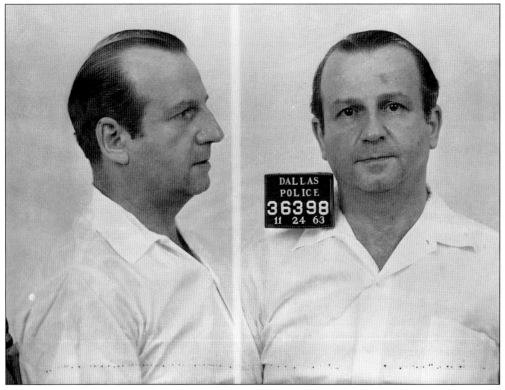

Apartment 207 at the Marsalis Apartments, at 223 Ewing Street, was Jack Ruby's home from 1962 to November 24, 1963. Ruby shared the apartment with George Senator, a drifter who helped out Ruby with odd jobs in lieu of rent and cared for his pet dachshunds. The interior of Ruby's apartment is seen at right as it was discovered by the Dallas Police Department in 1963. The apartment building is seen below in 1986, after it had become the Circle Inn. (Right, National Archives; below, Ed Zabel.)

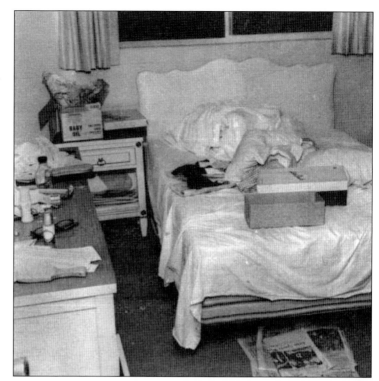

The Steak n Egg Kitchen, now a veterinary clinic at 1221 North Beckley Avenue, was two blocks from Oswald's rooming house on Beckley. Photographed here in 1986, the diner was called Dobbs House Restaurant in 1963. Waitress Mary Ada Dowling recalled that Oswald was a regular customer. On his last visit, she reported that he was unpleasant and used curse words regarding his order. Officer J.D. Tippit was also a regular, but there is no indication that they knew each other. (Ed Zabel.)

Austin's Barbecue was located at 2321 West Illinois Boulevard from 1949 until it was razed in 2002. Originally called the Bull Pen, Austin Cook purchased the business in 1957 and promoted brisket "as tender as ole Austin's heart." J.D. Tippit once worked there as a security guard. Due to tangential connections to Jack Ruby, Austin Cook was interviewed by the FBI, but they concluded later that any relationships were coincidental. (Ed Zabel.)

Five

OTHER SITES

Tourists and history buffs visiting Dallas often visit most of the sites previously described in this book. However, there are many other places in the Dallas–Fort Worth area that are equally intriguing and historically relevant. Some are off the beaten path, while others are just a few blocks away from the more famous destinations.

Many of the historic events of November 22–24, for example, occurred at the 1914 Dallas City Hall, a public building that has only recently been opened more to visitors. In it are the old offices of the Dallas Police Department, where Lee Harvey Oswald was incarcerated and interrogated. Its basement is where Oswald was gunned down by shadowy nightclub owner Jack Ruby. Many dozens of witnesses to the assassination were also interviewed there.

The Dallas Trade Mart was President Kennedy's destination after the downtown parade through Dealey Plaza. He was scheduled to give a speech to 2,600 people at a sold-out luncheon in the Grand Courtyard of the Market Center. Dallas Trade Mart was founded in 1957 by real estate mogul Trammell Crow. The four-building campus includes the World Trade Center, Trade Mart, International Trade Plaza, and Market Hall. Inside these buildings, nearly 2,300 permanent showrooms offer more than 35,000 product lines from manufacturers around the world. (Above, Donald Speck; below, Dallas Municipal Archives.)

The Dallas Market Center sign has remained the same since 1963. It is seen above on the day of the assassination, and at right in a more recent photograph. (Above, *Dallas Times-Herald*/Sixth Floor Museum at Dealey Plaza; right, Dallas Municipal Archives.)

00:16:01:09

The luncheon at the Trade Mart was organized by the Dallas Citizens Council; the Dallas Assembly, a civic leadership group; and the Graduate Research Center of the Southwest, later the University of Texas at Dallas. When Kennedy failed to arrive, attendees were asked to be patient. Upon learning that Kennedy was gravely wounded, J. Erik Jonsson, the cofounder of Texas Instruments and the future mayor of Dallas, relayed the sad news to a shocked room. (Sixth Floor Museum at Dealey Plaza.

In 1964, English sculptor Elisabeth Frink created this bronze sculpture, *The Eagle*, which sits outside the main entrance of the Trade Mart. It features a William Blake quote and a plaque that reads, "Placed in memorial by the friends of President John Fitzgerald Kennedy who awaited his arrival at the Dallas Trade Mart Nov. 22, 1963." The Blake quote is: "When thou seest an eagle/ thou seest a portion of genius/lift up thy head." (Dallas Municipal Archives.)

At the time of the assassination, Lee Harvey Oswald was separated from his wife, Marina. She and her children lived at the home of Ruth Paine, in this modest dwelling at 2515 West Fifth Street in Irving. Fluent in Russian, Paine made friends with Marina Oswald, who moved in with two small children. It was Paine who told Lee Harvey Oswald about a job opportunity at the Texas School Book Depository. The house is seen above in 1963, and below in the current day. (Above, National Archives; below, Irving City Archives.)

The garage at 2515 West Fifth Street still produces chills. Irving archivist Kevin Kendro recalled, "When the police came, Ruth Paine and Marina Oswald were in [the kitchen], and were asked, was there a rifle and Marina said, well yes, they did have one, so they came in here to get it. And there was just a rolled-up blanket. The rifle was gone." (National Archives.)

The City of Irving purchased the former Paine home in 2009 and is restoring it to its 1963 condition to be turned into a museum in time for the 50th anniversary of the Kennedy assassination, on November 22, 2013. The Irving City Archives coordinated the restoration and exhibits. (Irving City Archives.)

The Municipal Building, better known as the 1914 Dallas City Hall, is located at 2014 Main Street. The Beaux Arts–style building, designed by C.D. Hill, opened on October 17, 1914. It served as Dallas's city hall from 1914 to 1978, and included the police department and the city jail. The jail was on the top floor of the building. In 1963, the third floor housed the main offices of the police department. Lee Harvey Oswald spent the last 48 hours of life on these floors. (Both, Dallas Municipal Archives.)

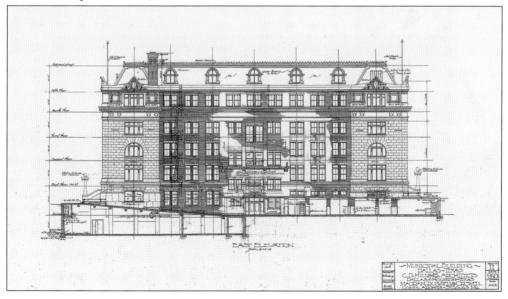

After his arrest in Oak Cliff, presumed Kennedy assassin Lee Harvey Oswald was taken to the third-floor offices of the homicide and robbery bureau and then to the office of homicide captain Will Fritz for the first of several interrogation sessions. After Captain Fritz charged Oswald with the murder of J.D. Tippit, Oswald was formally arraigned at 7:10 p.m. before Justice of the Peace David L. Johnston. (*Dallas Morning News.*)

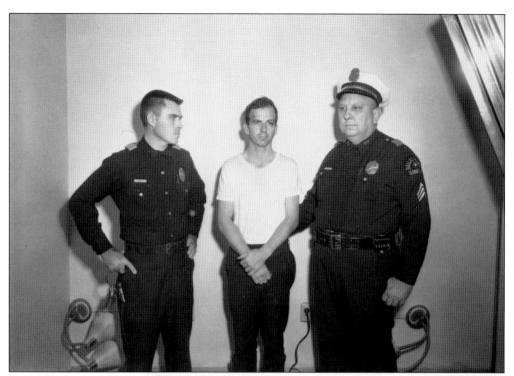

Oswald's mug shots were taken with minimal cooperation from Oswald. He is seen above with two wary police officers. At right is an enlargement from a slide transparency, which is perhaps the only known color image of Oswald in the city jail. (Both, Dallas Municipal Archives.)

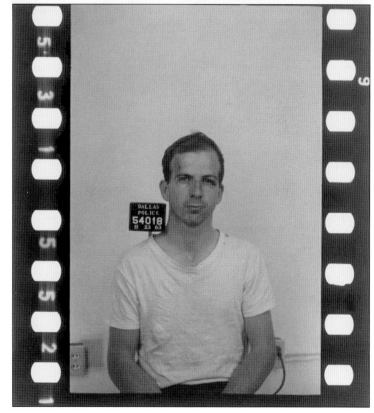

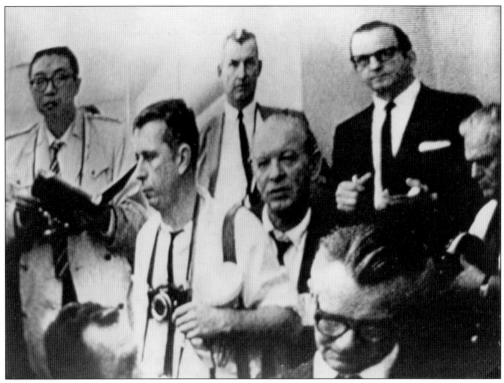

Shortly after midnight, detectives took Oswald to the basement assembly room for an appearance of several minutes before members of the press. Jack Ruby, Oswald's assassin, appears in the videotape of the crowded press conference, seen here, apparently impersonating a reporter. (Sixth Floor Museum at Dealey Plaza, WFAA collection.)

At about 12:20 a.m., Oswald was jailed in this maximum-security cell on the fifth floor of city hall. His cell was the center of a block of three cells separated from the primary jail area. (Dallas Municipal Archives.)

On Sunday morning, November 24, 1963, Oswald was scheduled to be transferred to the county jail. At 11:21 a.m., in full view of millions of television viewers, Jack Ruby lunged from the crowd of newsmen and policemen witnessing the transfer and shot Oswald once. Oswald was declared dead at Parkland Hospital at 1:07 p.m. (Sixth Floor Museum at Dealey Plaza, WFAA collection.)

The city jail basement of the old city hall has remained closed to tourists since Oswald was murdered there. The photograph above shows the processing station that Oswald and his jailers passed. The photograph below shows the ramp into the basement Jack Ruby walked down to approach Oswald. (Both, Dallas Municipal Archives.)

Both the Dallas Police Department and the Warren Commission investigations intensely examined how Jack Ruby gained access to the basement and how he got to Oswald. At right, KRLD reporter Bob Huffaker and a Dallas detective stand where Oswald was shot. Below, two Warren Commission members, John McCloy and Sen. John Cooper (first and third from the right), listen as Capt. Will Fritz (left, in hat) describes the scene. (Both, *Dallas Morning News*.)

The Western Union Building, at 2028–2034 Main Street, was built in 1913 as a Masonic lodge. The lodge used the building until 1919, and Western Union occupied it from 1919 to 1991. Designed by the Lang & Witchell architectural firm, the building exhibits Egyptian details. On Sunday, November 24, Jack Ruby walked to the Western Union office, where he wired $25 by telegraph to Karen Carlin, one of his strippers, in Fort Worth. The building is seen above in the current day. Below is a copy of the receipt for Ruby's money transaction. (Above, Dallas Municipal Archives; below, National Archives.)

In late 1959, Jack Ruby became a partner in the Sovereign, a private club at 1312 1/2 Commerce Street whose name was changed to the Carousel Club. It was one of three downtown Dallas burlesque clubs featuring strippers. All of the structures on that portion of Commerce Street were condemned in 1973 and demolished to build the Southwestern Bell office complex, which is now AT&T Plaza. (At right, National Archives; below, Dallas Municipal Archives.)

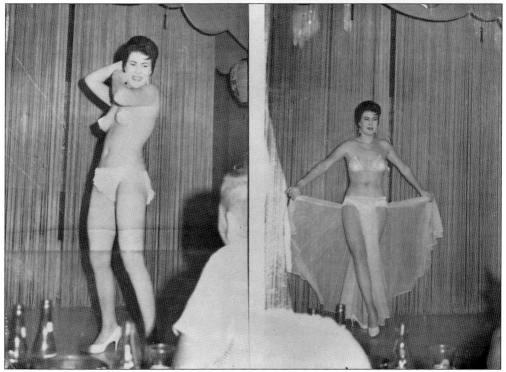

Late in 1963, Ruby began to distribute passes to the Carousel. His business card is seen above. Ruby was known for his hot temper. Once, during a scuffle, the top half of his left index finger was bitten and later amputated. The fingerprint card below shows the missing digit. (Both, Dallas Municipal Archives.)

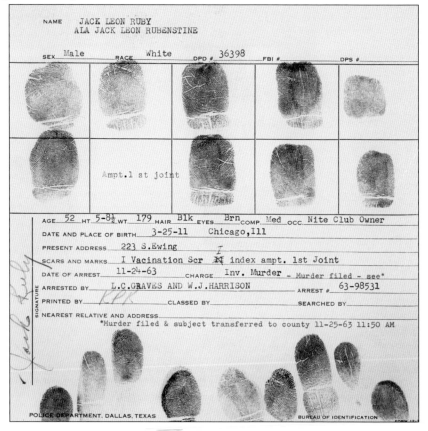

One of the buildings bordering Dealey Plaza on the east is the Dallas County Criminal Courts Building (right). Built in 1915 at the northeast corner of Main and Houston Streets, it once counted as residents Clyde Barrow and the gangster Charles Arthur "Pretty Boy" Floyd. It was where Lee Harvey Oswald was being transferred when he was gunned down in the city jail basement by Jack Ruby on November 24, 1963. Ruby (below) was then incarcerated here, and his trial was held in one of the courtrooms on the second floor. (Right, Dallas Heritage Village; below, Dallas Municipal Archives.)

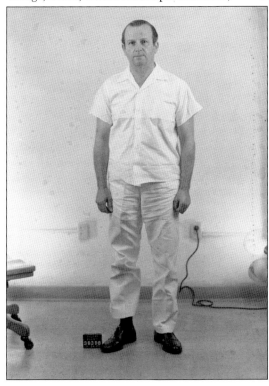

Jack Ruby was held in the Dallas County Criminal Courts Building and tried there for Oswald's murder in the court of Judge Joe B. Brown. Some believe that Ruby killed Oswald to keep him from revealing a larger conspiracy, though Ruby denied the charge, maintaining that he was acting out of patriotism. In March 1964, he was found guilty and sentenced to death. He died of a pulmonary embolism when his case was still on appeal in 1967. Above is Ruby's bond hearing in December 1963. Ruby is seen below, in the backseat of the car, arriving for the trial in January 1964. (Both, *Dallas Morning News*.)

Jack Ruby's trial was watched closely, chronicled by 200 reporters from across the globe. This image is from February 10, 1964. (*Dallas Morning News.*)

This is the courtroom of Judge J. Frank Wilson, who made his facilities available to Judge Joe B. Brown for Ruby's trial. Brown's court seated only 67, whereas Wilson's accommodated 200. (*Dallas Morning News.*)

Prospective jurors for the Ruby trial are seen above waiting in the central jury room in the Dallas County Courts Building. (*Dallas Morning News.*)

The members of the Ruby jury are seen here. They found Ruby guilty of murder, and sentenced him to death in the electric chair. He died of a pulmonary embolism associated with lung cancer while the case was on appeal in 1967. (*Dallas Morning News.*)

Old and New County Courthouses with Kennedy Memorial - Dallas

Dallas civic leaders wrestled emotionally about how to honor the slain President Kennedy. Philip Johnson, an architect and Kennedy family friend, was selected to design a memorial. The John F. Kennedy Memorial Plaza is located one block east of Dealey Plaza, between Main and Commerce Streets, on land donated by Dallas County. (Dallas Heritage Village.)

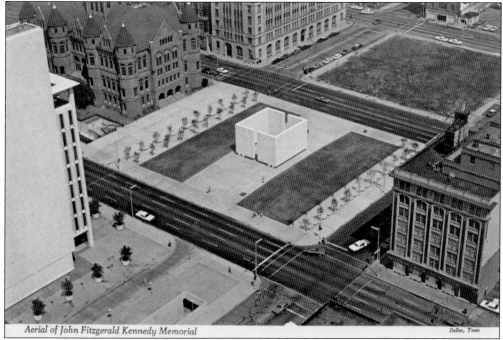

Aerial of John Fitzgerald Kennedy Memorial Dallas, Texas

The Kennedy memorial was the first memorial designed by Philip Johnson and was approved by Jacqueline Kennedy. Johnson called it "a place of quiet refuge, an enclosed place of thought and contemplation separated from the city around, but near the sky and earth." The cenotaph and the surrounding square, funded entirely by citizens, were dedicated on June 24, 1970. (*Dallas Morning News.*)

This home, at 4011 Turtle Creek Boulevard, belonged to Maj. Gen. Edwin Walker. Marina Oswald testified to the Warren Commission that her husband confessed to her in April 1963 that he unsuccessfully attempted to assassinate Walker, who was an outspoken anticommunist and segregationist. Marina Oswald told the Warren Commission that Lee considered Walker the leader of a "fascist organization." (Ed Zabel.)

Lee Harvey Oswald fired at Walker through a window from less than 100 feet away, but Walker's only injury was bullet fragments to the forearm. Before the Kennedy assassination, Dallas police had no suspects in the Walker shooting. A note that Oswald left for Marina on the night of the attempt on Walker's life, instructing her what to do if he did not return, was found in early December 1963. (National Archives.)

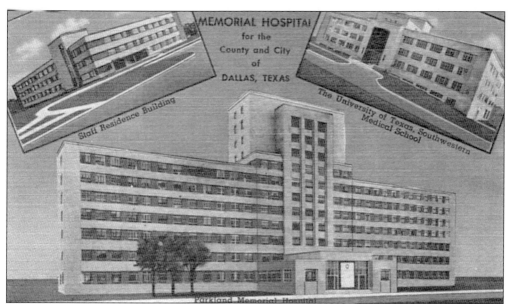

Parkland Memorial Hospital is located at 5201 Harry Hines Boulevard. It is the main hospital of the Parkland Health & Hospital System and serves as Dallas County's public hospital. President Kennedy was pronounced dead there on November 22, 1963. The postcard above is from about 1955. (Dallas Municipal Archives.)

Parkland was originally the city-county hospital, and it now ranks among the largest teaching hospitals in the nation. Texas Woman's University began its bachelor of science in nursing program at Parkland in 1954 and still serves as the major teaching hospital of the University of Texas Southwestern Medical Center. Its trauma center is recognized internationally. This view is believed to be from 1963. (*Dallas Morning News.*)

The president's limousine arrived at Parkland at 12:38 p.m. More than a dozen Parkland doctors and nurses in Trauma Room One employed all of their resources to save Kennedy's life, but the wounds were too grave to treat. The image above shows the activity outside Parkland on that day. (*Dallas Morning News.*)

Gov. John Connally was also wounded, with an entry wound in his back, a broken rib, an exit wound in his chest, a shattered wrist, and a fragment lodged in his thigh. This photograph shows a bouquet of roses on the floor of one of the motorcade limousines outside Parkland on November 22. It was not the president's car. (*Dallas Morning News.*)

As soon as the news broke, the concerned and the curious descended on Parkland and held vigil outside the emergency area. Citizens poured out their grief after the sad news was announced. (*Dallas Morning News.*)

At 1:33 p.m., acting White House press secretary Malcolm Kilduff entered a nurses' classroom at the hospital filled with press reporters and made the official announcement of the president's death. (*Dallas Morning News.*)

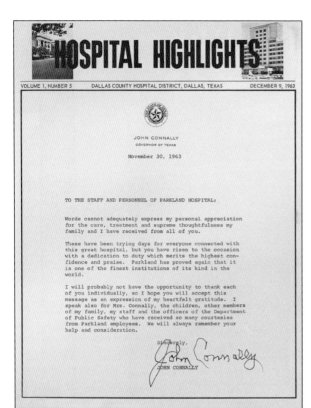

HOSPITAL HIGHLIGHTS

VOLUME 1, NUMBER 5   DALLAS COUNTY HOSPITAL DISTRICT, DALLAS, TEXAS   DECEMBER 9, 1963

JOHN CONNALLY
GOVERNOR OF TEXAS

November 30, 1963

TO THE STAFF AND PERSONNEL OF PARKLAND HOSPITAL:

Words cannot adequately express my personal appreciation
for the care, treatment and supreme thoughtfulness my
family and I have received from all of you.

These have been trying days for everyone connected with
this great hospital, but you have risen to the occasion
with a dedication to duty which merits the highest con-
fidence and praise. Parkland has proved again that it
is one of the finest institutions of its kind in the
world.

I will probably not have the opportunity to thank each
of you individually, so I hope you will accept this
message as an expression of my heartfelt gratitude. I
speak also for Mrs. Connally, the children, other members
of my family, my staff and the officers of the Department
of Public Safety who have received so many courtesies
from Parkland employees. We will always remember your
help and consideration.

Sincerely,

John Connally
JOHN CONNALLY

In this letter, published in the Parkland Hospital newsletter, Governor Connally thanked the staff for their professional treatment and grace under pressure. (University of Texas Southwestern Medical School Archives.)

Two days after the assassination, Lee Harvey Oswald was rushed to Parkland after being shot in the abdomen by Jack Ruby, and died in Operating Room Five after more than 90 minutes of surgery. Ruby died on January 3, 1967, in the same emergency room, from a pulmonary embolism associated with lung cancer. In the screen capture below from WBAP-TV (now KXAS), Dr. Tom Shires announces Oswald's death to the media. (KXAS-TV.)

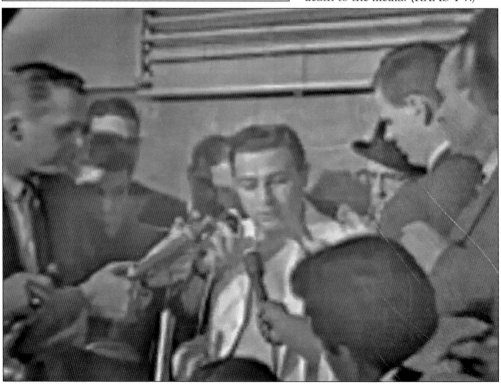

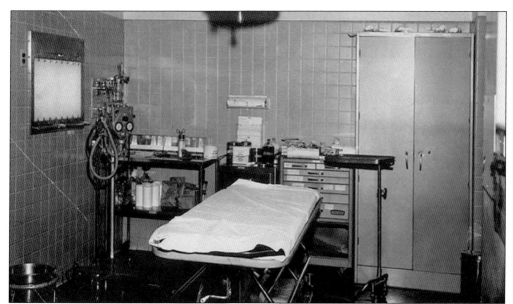

Parkland Memorial Hospital has expanded and changed significantly since 1963. The original emergency room, seen here, now makes up Parkland's radiology department. Trauma Room One was dismantled and purchased by the National Archives along with the contents of the room. Today, a plaque at Parkland marks the original site of Trauma Room One. (University of Texas Southwestern Medical School Archives.)

On January 17, 1964, the Dallas Garden Center planted this sturdy Success-variety pecan tree with help from the Dallas Park Board and the Dallas Park Department. Today, 49 years later, the pecan is still standing on the west side of Ranger Circle, adjacent to the Discovery Gardens. (Dallas Municipal Archives.)

DISCOVER THOUSANDS OF LOCAL HISTORY BOOKS FEATURING MILLIONS OF VINTAGE IMAGES

Arcadia Publishing, the leading local history publisher in the United States, is committed to making history accessible and meaningful through publishing books that celebrate and preserve the heritage of America's people and places.

Find more books like this at
www.arcadiapublishing.com

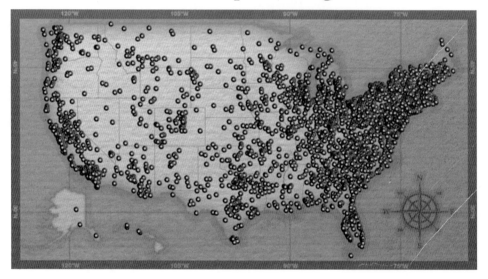

Search for your hometown history, your old stomping grounds, and even your favorite sports team.

Consistent with our mission to preserve history on a local level, this book was printed in South Carolina on American-made paper and manufactured entirely in the United States. Products carrying the accredited Forest Stewardship Council (FSC) label are printed on 100 percent FSC-certified paper.

MADE IN THE USA